BUSH BEAUTIES

COLLECTORS EDITION

JILLIAN SAWYER

Photography & Graphics
WAYNE McONIE

Photography
CHRIS GARNETT

Published by
GLASS BOOKS PTY LTD

Printed in Western Australia

This edition is dedicated to my husband and daughter, Brian and Kerin,

for their unfaltering love

and

to a dynamic duo, Wayne and Yvonne.

National Library of Australia Cataloguing-in-Publication entry

Sawyer, Jillian.
Bush beauties.

Collectors ed.
ISBN 0 9585282 9 2.

1. Glass craft - Patterns. 2. Glass painting and staining - Patterns. 3. Decoration and ornament - Animal forms - Australia. 4. Decoration and ornament - Plant forms - Australia. I. McOnie, Wayne.
II. Sawyer, Jillian. Australian bush beauties. III. Sawyer, Jillian. More bush beauties. IV. Title.

748.5

Published by Glass Books Pty Ltd
PO Box 891 Subiaco Western Australia 6904
sales@glassbooks.com.au
www.glassbooks.com.au
March 2003
Reprinted June 2004

FOREWORD

Hi!

In Australia, we have vast areas of untamed wilderness. Thousands of miles of harsh unforgiving country, sunburnt arid interior, lush seasonal wetlands, spectacular gorges, awesome outcrops, and always, always, the impression of age beyond old. This is the Great Australian Outback!

Generally just called *The Outback,* Aussies typically refer to these remote areas as:
The Back of Beyond – a very long way from anywhere.
The Back of Nowhere – even further away.
Never Never Land – remote outback.
Beyond the Black Stump – a long, long way from anything, or just
The Bush – the hinterland, the outback, anywhere that isn't in town.

To further define *The Bush* you'll also need to know these terms:
The Back Blocks – the outer suburbs.
Out in the Sticks – out in the country, beyond the *Back Blocks.*

So, in the outer suburbs or in the country, the bush can start right outside your back fence with all the delightful bush flora and fauna to go with it.

Now, welcome to *BUSH BEAUTIES Collectors Edition* which is a compilation of two earlier books, *AUSTRALIAN BUSH BEAUTIES* and *MORE BUSH BEAUTIES.*

To those of you who are familiar with these books, I am sure you will enjoy this bigger, brighter, better version. To those who aren't familiar with these productions, welcome to this Bush experience and remember, in Australia, the phrase *just down the road* can mean anything from a couple of hundred yards to a couple of hundred miles!

JILLIAN SAWYER

PO Box 522
Cannington
Western Australia 6107
Email: firebird@iinet.net.au

PS When Aussies want to get away from it all, we say they've *Gone Outback, Gone Walkabout, Gone off the Beaten Track* or just *GONE BUSH.*

GALAH

LAUGHING KOOKABURRAS

BARN OWL

KOALA

GALAH

*Flocks of these much-loved birds
are a sight to behold as they bank
and wheel in pink and grey clouds.*

LAUGHING KOOKABURRAS

*A complex family social system helps
to regulate a low birth rate in keeping
with a longevity of 20 years. Young are
not driven away and stay to help defend
the territory and rear and protect the
offspring. By occupying areas that would
otherwise be taken over by potential
breeders, they reduce the birthrate by
about one third. This system improves
the chances of survival for all members
of the family.*

BARN OWL

Small mammals, insects, mice and birds are targeted during the Barn Owl's silent flight.

KOALA

This harmless and lovable marsupial ranges from the tropics to the cool, temperate regions of eastern Australia. Hunted for their pelts, they were almost wiped out until re-established by nature lovers. Ongoing research will help to ensure this endearing species will continue to survive.

QUEEN OF SHEBA ORCHID

CAPER WHITE BUTTERFLY

9

QUEEN OF SHEBA ORCHID

Justice cannot be done to this truly exquisite orchid. The outer petals are purple, with crimson and gold borders, and the inner petals blue-purple with the whole being streaked and dotted with darker tones.

As with other sun orchids, the flowers open only on warm sunny days.

CAPER WHITE BUTTERFLY

In spite of their restricted food preferences they are common, widespread and found throughout Australia. Adults are migratory and vast numbers may be seen flying together.

RAINBOW BEE-EATER

AZURE KINGFISHER

GOULDIAN FINCH

STAGHORN FERN

GIANT OR BLUE WATERLILY

ROTHS TREE FROG

RAINBOW BEE-EATER

These beautifully coloured birds specialise in taking dragonflies and other insects on the wing or off the surface of water, carefully removing the stings before eating.

AZURE KINGFISHER

One of only two Australian kingfishers that are exclusively hunters of aquatic prey, the Azure Kingfisher gathers food from the rivers, creeks and estuaries of the wetland. With Australia being so arid, kingfishers have been able to inhabit the rest of the continent only by developing dry land hunting habits.

GOULDIAN FINCHES

This most striking of all Australian grass finches has three colour forms, the most common being the black headed, the red headed in minority and, rarely, the yellow headed.

STAGHORN FERN

The infertile backing fronds help attach the fern to its host and act as collectors for food. As they die they help to create a peat-like area which the roots of the fern penetrate to obtain sustenance and moisture. The fertile fronds overhang and produce patches of spore, then die and fall off, to be replaced by fresh fronds.

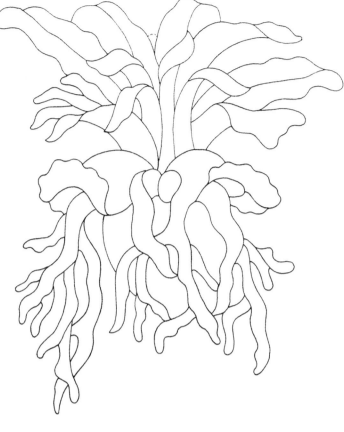

GIANT OR BLUE WATERLILY

Its habitat is the east coast from northern Queensland to northern New South Wales in still water in rivers and ponds. Flowers can be blue to mauve, pink or white with yellow centres.

ROTHS TREE FROG

These frogs are capable of a striking colour change from rich mottled brown, to an even, very pale cream - almost white. They are found in the Kimberley region of northern Western Australia. The eye colouring (red upper iris and pale metallic gold lower) is found only in Roths Tree Frog and its close relatives.

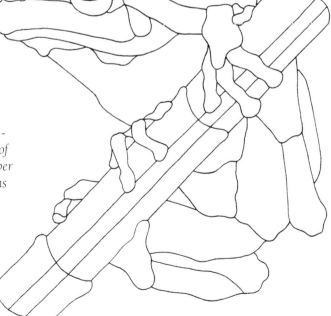

SPLENDID WREN

PARAKEELYA AND COPPERCUPS

ULYSSES BUTTERFLY

HEART-LEAF FLAME PEA

COOKTOWN ORCHID

SPLENDID WREN

SPLENDID WREN

*The male, in full breeding plumage, is the most beautiful
and unforgettable of the blue wren. Not easy to spot as it
forages quickly through low heartland shrubs, this shy bird
will not readily accept the presence of humans.*

ULYSSES BUTTERFLY

*The Ulysses is one of the largest of Australia's
butterflies and favours the outskirts of rainforests.*

PARAKEELYA AND COPPERCUPS

*Their habitat is sandy soils in arid areas.
Parakeelya are the larger flower here
and Coppercups the smaller flower and buds.*

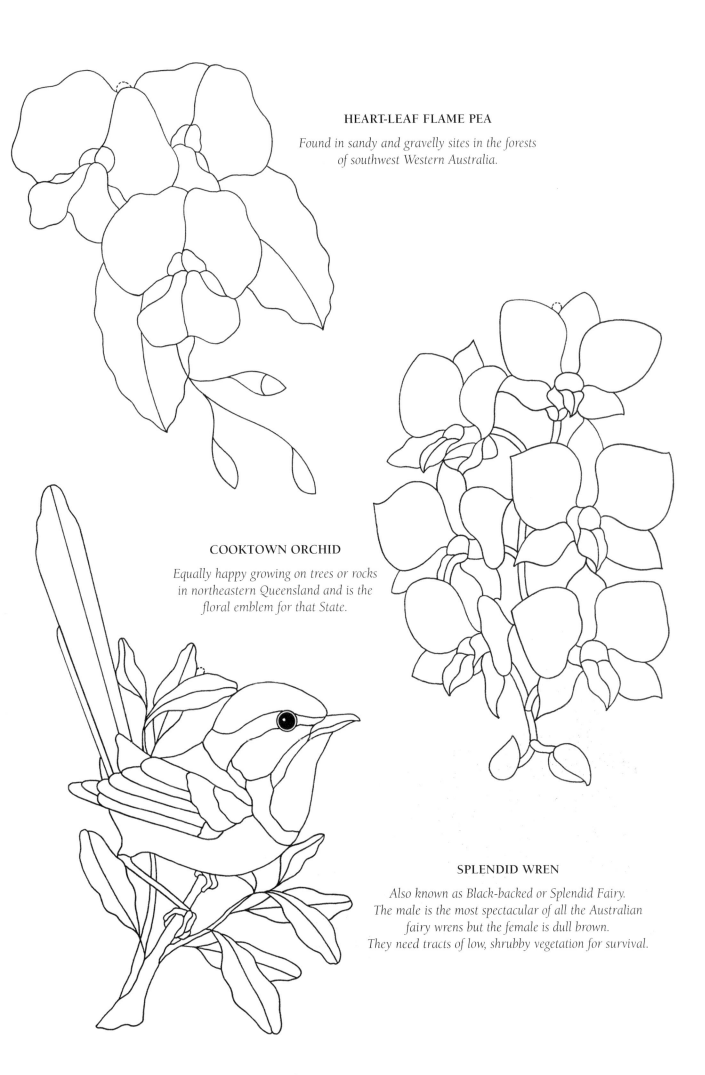

HEART-LEAF FLAME PEA

*Found in sandy and gravelly sites in the forests
of southwest Western Australia.*

COOKTOWN ORCHID

*Equally happy growing on trees or rocks
in northeastern Queensland and is the
floral emblem for that State.*

SPLENDID WREN

*Also known as Black-backed or Splendid Fairy.
The male is the most spectacular of all the Australian
fairy wrens but the female is dull brown.
They need tracts of low, shrubby vegetation for survival.*

FUSCHIA GUM

RAINBOW LORIKEETS

20

ELECTUS PARROTS

RED FLOWERED TEMPLETONIA

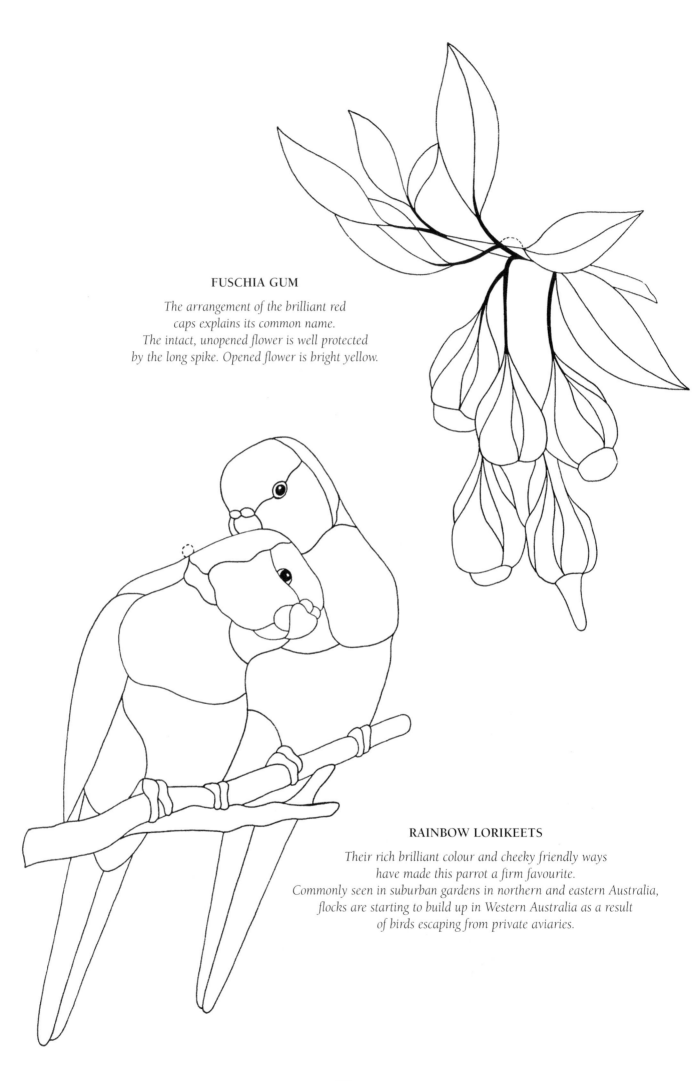

FUSCHIA GUM

*The arrangement of the brilliant red
caps explains its common name.
The intact, unopened flower is well protected
by the long spike. Opened flower is bright yellow.*

RAINBOW LORIKEETS

*Their rich brilliant colour and cheeky friendly ways
have made this parrot a firm favourite.
Commonly seen in suburban gardens in northern and eastern Australia,
flocks are starting to build up in Western Australia as a result
of birds escaping from private aviaries.*

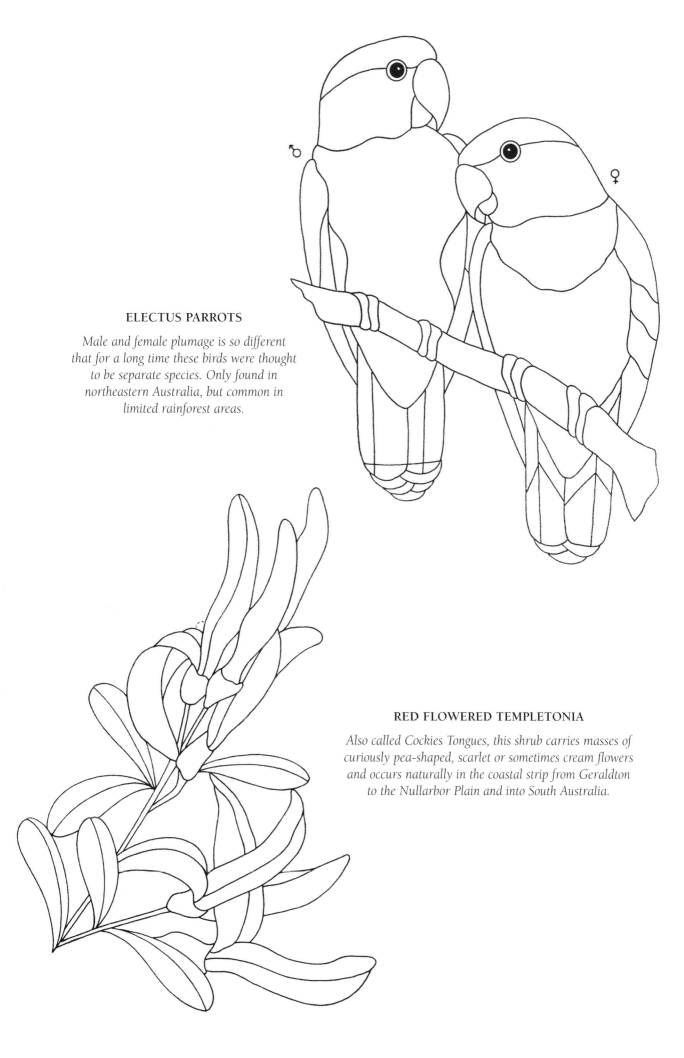

ELECTUS PARROTS

Male and female plumage is so different that for a long time these birds were thought to be separate species. Only found in northeastern Australia, but common in limited rainforest areas.

RED FLOWERED TEMPLETONIA

Also called Cockies Tongues, this shrub carries masses of curiously pea-shaped, scarlet or sometimes cream flowers and occurs naturally in the coastal strip from Geraldton to the Nullarbor Plain and into South Australia.

KING PARROTS

GREEN ROSELLA

BLACK SWAN

BLUE CHINA ORCHID   BLUE LECHENAULTIA

KING PARROTS

These stunning parrots are usually seen in pairs or small parties. Feeding mainly in the trees on seeds, fruits, berries, nuts and blossoms, they also come to the ground for fallen matter.

GREEN ROSELLA

Common in the woods of Tasmania and some offshore islands, these birds are not shy and are often seen in gardens. Favoured food source in winter is the berries of the introduced Hawthorn.

BLACK SWAN

Inhabits eastern and western parts of the continent, only venturing into central regions when rain fills inland lakes. Its nest is a huge floating heap of vegetation, usually on lakes and swamps.

BLUE CHINA ORCHID

Widespread in the southwest of Western Australia, these lovely orchids are an example of nature's ability to produce blue flowers of unsurpassed beauty.

BLUE LECHENAULTIA

One of Western Australia's best-known wildflowers, with its profusion of breathtaking blue flowers, few plants can equal its delicacy of texture. Colour ranges from pale azure to deep ultramarine, with rare white flowering forms.

PRINCESS PARROTS

SCARLET CHESTED PARROT

28

KANGAROOS

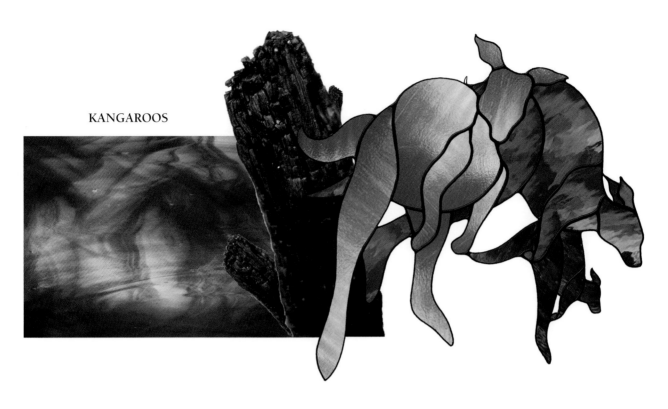

FRILLED-NECK LIZARD

29

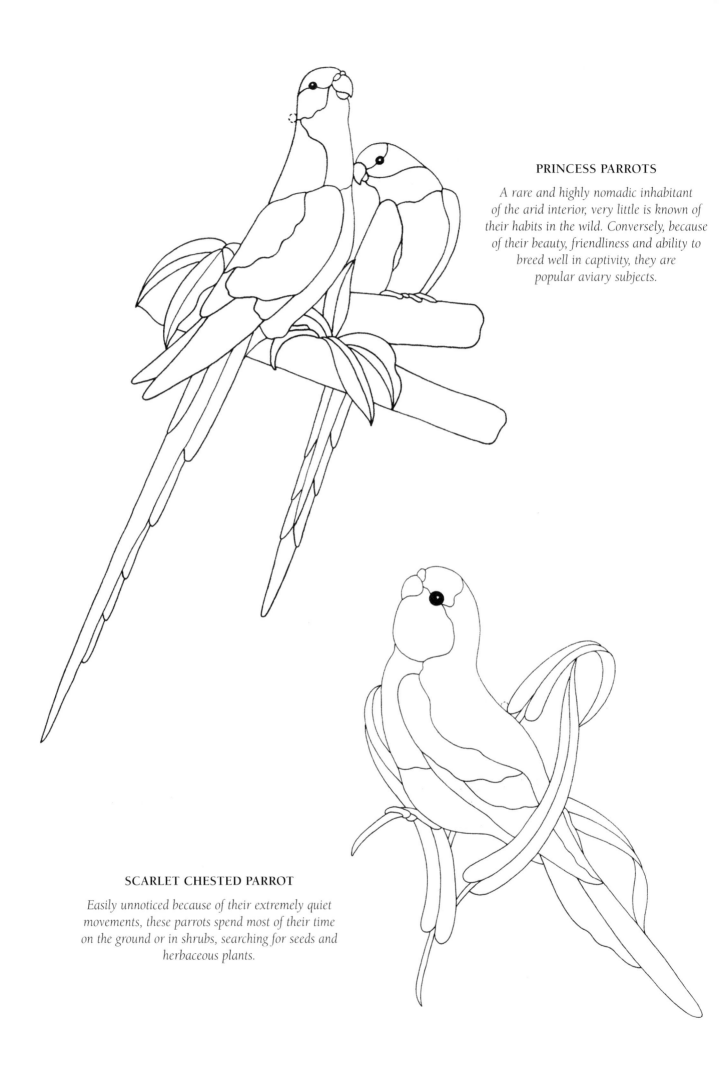

PRINCESS PARROTS

*A rare and highly nomadic inhabitant
of the arid interior, very little is known of
their habits in the wild. Conversely, because
of their beauty, friendliness and ability to
breed well in captivity, they are
popular aviary subjects.*

SCARLET CHESTED PARROT

*Easily unnoticed because of their extremely quiet
movements, these parrots spend most of their time
on the ground or in shrubs, searching for seeds and
herbaceous plants.*

KANGAROOS

There are approximately 48 species of kangaroos, wallabies and their relatives, collectively known as macropods (big feet), Australia wide. Few sights equal the grandeur of a mob of roos thundering over a sea of yellow grass or a desert of red sand.

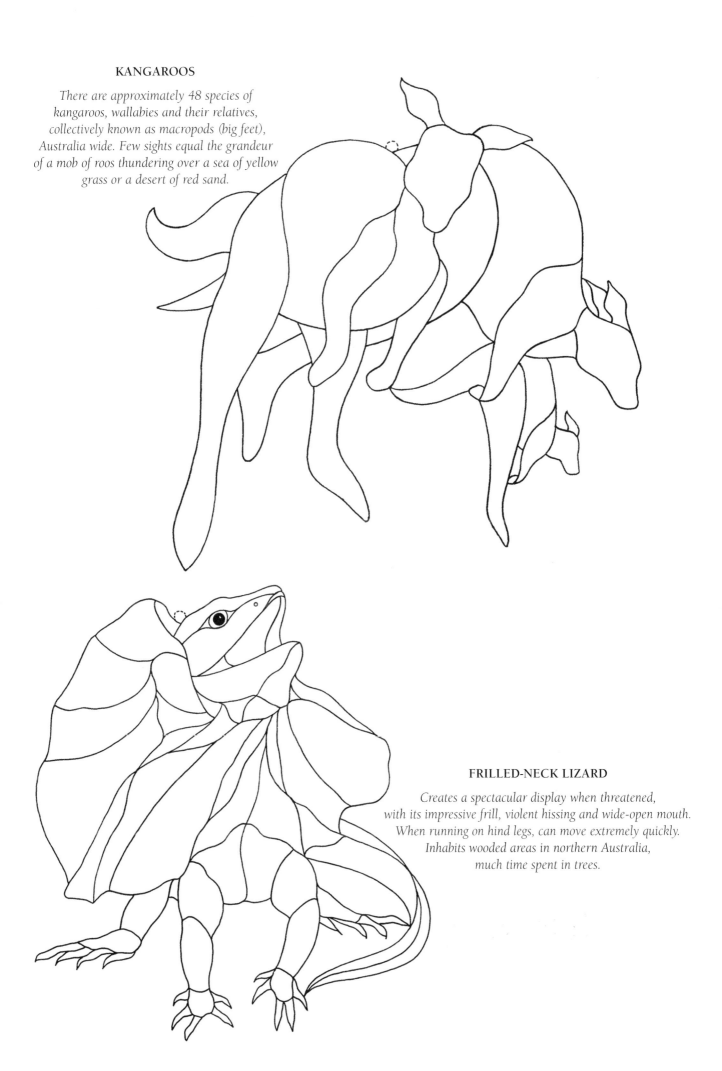

FRILLED-NECK LIZARD

Creates a spectacular display when threatened, with its impressive frill, violent hissing and wide-open mouth. When running on hind legs, can move extremely quickly. Inhabits wooded areas in northern Australia, much time spent in trees.

KANGAROO APPLE

NATIVE ROSELLA

LACE BARK

LEATHERWOOD

KANGAROO APPLE

*Inhabits wet forests and rainforest margins
in Queensland, New South Wales and Victoria.*

NATIVE ROSELLA

*Inhabits rainforest margins, tall forests and
riverbanks of the coast and tablelands of
the east coast of Australia.*

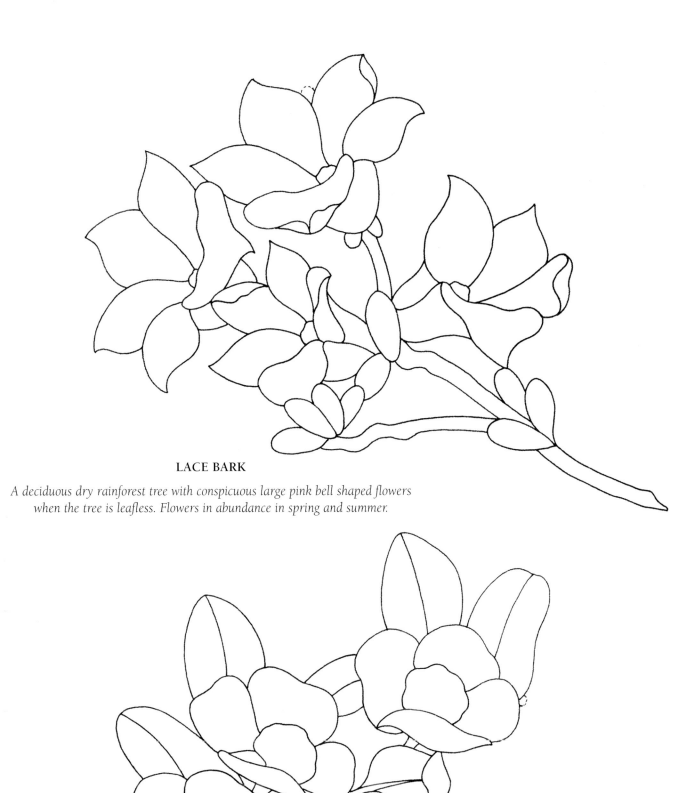

LACE BARK

A deciduous dry rainforest tree with conspicuous large pink bell shaped flowers when the tree is leafless. Flowers in abundance in spring and summer.

LEATHERWOOD

Endemic to Tasmania, the Leatherwood trees have masses of fragrant four-petalled, white flowers.

RED-CAPPED PARROT

GALAH

BRUSH TAILED PHASCOGALE

HONEY POSSUM

RED-CAPPED PARROT

VARIEGATED WREN

RED-CAPPED PARROT

Restricted to the southwest of Western Australia, these parrots have a very long upper beak that enables them to extract seed from the large fruit of the Marri tree (Eucalyptus Calophylla). Rarely seen far from Marri, their dependence on one species of tree makes them very vulnerable to loss of habitat.

GALAH

Such a common sight in Australia, their beauty is often unnoticed or taken for granted. Seedeaters, they gather nearly all their food from the ground. Quite large flocks are often seen in city and suburban parks. Flock feeding provides the advantages of more efficient food finding and greater safety.

BRUSH TAILED PHASCOGALE

This small carnivorous marsupial is mainly nocturnal, returning to a nest in a tree hollow to sleep in the day. The energy expended by the males in competition prior to mating, leaves them susceptible to stress related disease and they die soon afterwards.

HONEY POSSUM

This tiny possum has no close relatives and appears to be the sole survivor of an extinct group of marsupials. It lives only the southwest of Western Australia and has a long tubular snout and brush tipped tongue to enable it to probe the blossoms of the eucalyptus in search of nectar.

RED-CAPPED PARROT

A gaudy mixture of colours makes this parrot one of the most colourful of Australian birds. Sometimes know as the 'hookbill' because of the very long point to its upper bill, this parrot is found in the southwestern corner of Western Australia.

VARIEGATED WREN

The glittering blues, the chestnut, black and white areas give this lovely wren its name. Variegated Wrens build a small domed nest, sometimes only centimetres above the ground and feed on insects caught on the ground or from foliage.

39

LONG-TAILED PYGMY POSSUM

LEADBEATERS OR FAIRY POSSUM

BRUSH CHERRY

40

SULPHUR-CRESTED COCKATOO

ILLYARRIE

AUSTRALIAN MAGPIE

41

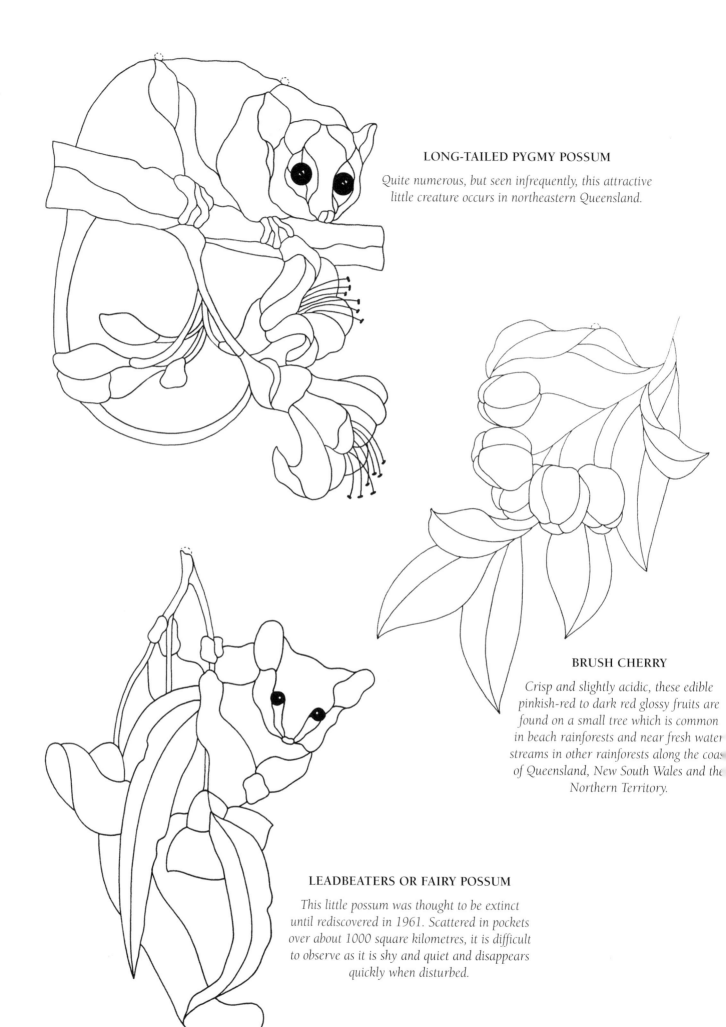

LONG-TAILED PYGMY POSSUM

Quite numerous, but seen infrequently, this attractive little creature occurs in northeastern Queensland.

BRUSH CHERRY

Crisp and slightly acidic, these edible pinkish-red to dark red glossy fruits are found on a small tree which is common in beach rainforests and near fresh water streams in other rainforests along the coas of Queensland, New South Wales and the Northern Territory.

LEADBEATERS OR FAIRY POSSUM

This little possum was thought to be extinct until rediscovered in 1961. Scattered in pockets over about 1000 square kilometres, it is difficult to observe as it is shy and quiet and disappears quickly when disturbed.

SULPHUR-CRESTED COCKATOO

Common and familiar in northern and eastern Australia with raucous screech advertising their presence and sounding a noisy alarm if disturbed.

ILLYARRIE

The bright red bud-caps contrast well with the outstanding yellow mass-stamened flowers.

AUSTRALIAN MAGPIE

Well known, boldly marked black and white species. Fierce when nesting and will attack humans in defence of its territory.

SULPHUR-CRESTED COCKATOO

BLUE MOUNTAIN TREE FROG

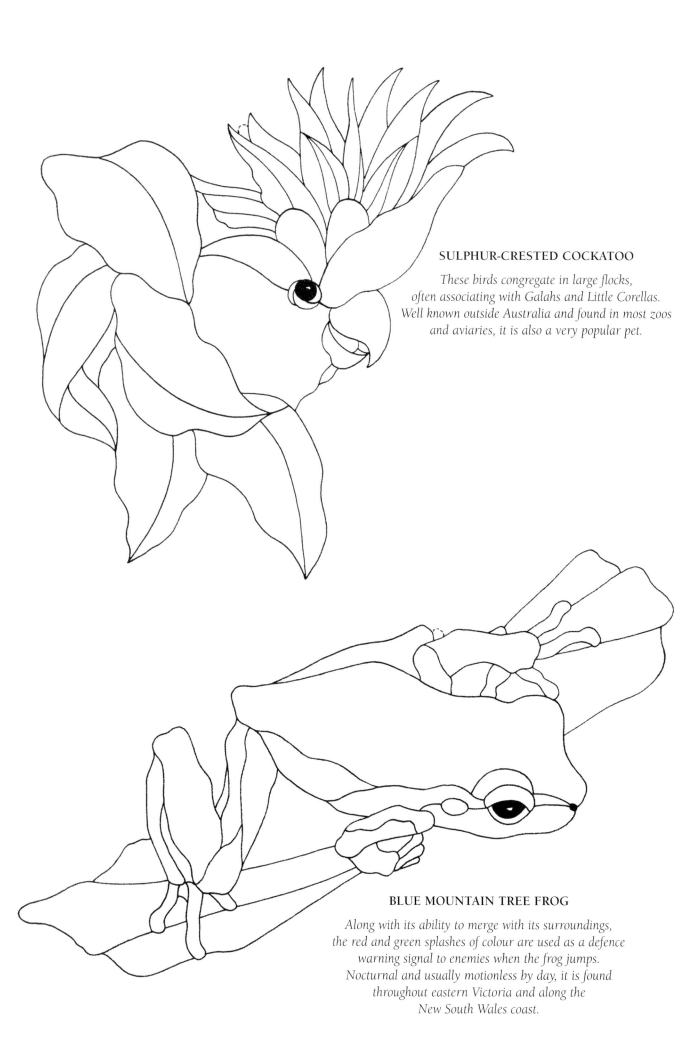

SULPHUR-CRESTED COCKATOO

*These birds congregate in large flocks,
often associating with Galahs and Little Corellas.
Well known outside Australia and found in most zoos
and aviaries, it is also a very popular pet.*

BLUE MOUNTAIN TREE FROG

*Along with its ability to merge with its surroundings,
the red and green splashes of colour are used as a defence
warning signal to enemies when the frog jumps.
Nocturnal and usually motionless by day, it is found
throughout eastern Victoria and along the
New South Wales coast.*

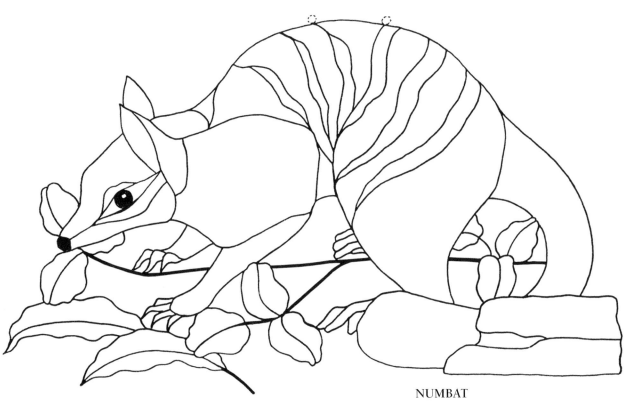

NUMBAT

Under threat of extinction this pretty, carnivorous marsupial,
with a tail like a bottlebrush and an appetite for termites,
is now found only in a small area of southwestern Australia.

PLATYPUS

Few people are lucky enough to see this improbable and
unique Australian mammal in the wild. Though it is quite common,
it is also vulnerable due to loss of habitat.

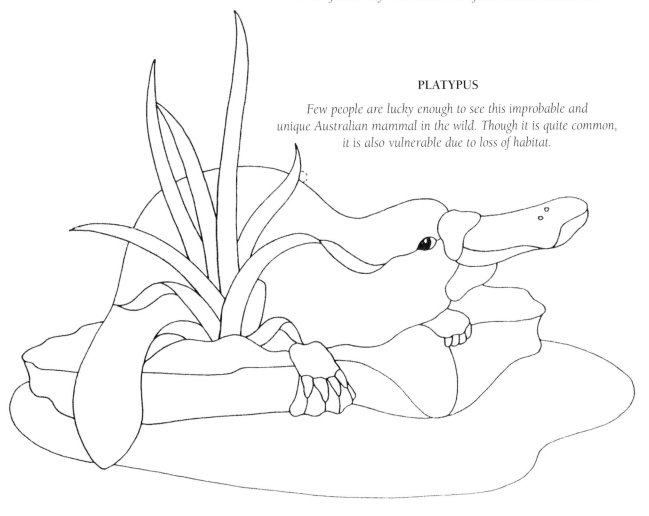

RED-EYED TREE FROG

WHITE-WINGED WREN

48

LUMHOLTZ'S TREE KANGAROO

RED LACEWING BUTTERFLY

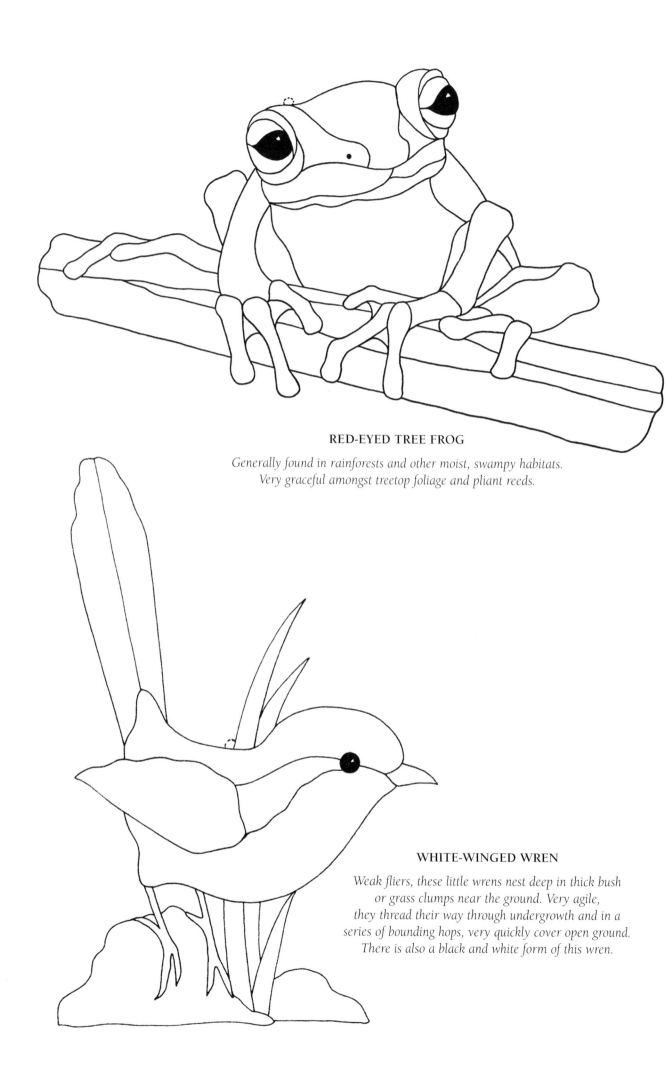

RED-EYED TREE FROG

*Generally found in rainforests and other moist, swampy habitats.
Very graceful amongst treetop foliage and pliant reeds.*

WHITE-WINGED WREN

*Weak fliers, these little wrens nest deep in thick bush
or grass clumps near the ground. Very agile,
they thread their way through undergrowth and in a
series of bounding hops, very quickly cover open ground.
There is also a black and white form of this wren.*

LUMHOLTZ'S TREE KANGAROO

This nocturnal kangaroo spends its days sleeping in a crouched sitting position in a branch in the crown of a rainforest tree. An efficient climber, it would be greatly aided by a prehensile tail but, as with other kangaroos, its tail is used only as a counter balance.

RED LACEWING BUTTERFLY

Of the family Nymphalidae, this lovely butterfly inhabits the forest of northeast Queensland. Its larvae are black with yellow stripes and long branched black spines.

51

AZURE KINGFISH

AUSTRALIAN
BIRDWING

AZURE KINGFISHER

*Spends much of its time perched on a branch, usually not more
than a metre above water. Here it sits quietly staring into
the water, head bobbing excitedly if suitable prey appears.
Then it dives down in a flash of blue, seizes the prey and flies
back to the branch to feed. The kingfisher then reverts
to its watching position, waiting for more fish, insects or
crustaceans to appear.*

AUSTRALIAN BIRDWING

The largest Australian butterfly, the Birdwing is also one of the largest in the world. The female's wings may span 200mm (8 inches). Birdwings normally inhabit rainforests and are butterflies of the air, flying high around the tops of rainforest trees.

RED-BACK SPIDER

Known in Russia as the Black Wolf and America as the Black Widow, in Australia this spider with its sinister beauty has been immortalised in song for its habit of lurking in outback dunnies* and inflicting painful, and sometimes deadly, bites in embarrassing places.

*Australian slang for toilet

RED-BACK SPIDER